A Counselor's
Poetic Guide

Through the Grief Journey

Natalie Ross, LPC-S

Leena Enterprises

Leena Enterprises LLC

Arlington, TX 76016

Cover Design by Ariel Perez Benino

Printed in the United States of America

ISBN: 978-1-7362047-0-2 (paperback)

ISBN: 978-1-7362047-1-9 (eBook)

This book is dedicated to everyone who has endured a death loss (with especial warmth to my fellow "Angel Parents" who have had to bury a child) and the members of my "Good Grief" group.

TABLE OF CONTENTS

CHAPTER EIGHT

OTHERS

ABOUT

My words used to hide in my chest like the extremities of a turtle in uncharted territories. Like many of you, writing poetry as a child and adolescent helped me express myself and overcome being shy. In high school, two friends and I collaborated on a poem about family trauma and death loss. The piece brought our classroom to tears and revealed to me the moving power of words.

For the next decade, life happenings took precedence over my writing. However, when my son Nathaniel "Peanut" died, I desperately needed to unhook from the anchor of despair. Poetry was my expressive homeland. Now, the prodigal daughter, I found my way back to writing. The healing power of spoken word became clear when I expanded beyond writing poems to performing at open mic events. The mutual support we created, as we shared the underbelly parts of our circumstances, filled me with hope.

It was my destiny to help others. My mom says, as an infant, I motivated her to heal through grief. Growing up, you could always find me sticking up for my disabled friend, advocating for my brother and picking up his chores, cleaning matter out of animals' eyes, showing the new kids around, or assisting my teachers. After high school, I took a step to submit to my calling by pursuing my B.A. in Psychology from the University of Texas at San Antonio in 2008.

During my study there, the Children's Bereavement Center of South Texas (CBCST) gave me an exceptional training and work opportunity to serve families who had endured situations that were too overwhelming to verbally process. Using expressive arts like writing and painting helped. These experiences developed my passion for working with grieving youth and families.

I obtained my master's degree in Community Counseling in 2010 from St. Mary's University. My professors were brilliant. My time working with youth, adults, and families who suffered trauma was priceless. Upon receiving my full counseling license in 2014, Dallas-Fort Worth became my new home.

After working as a Youth Trauma Counselor for a couple of years, I co-opened my current counseling practice Walk of Life Wellness Center. Although I loved my role, the helper in me craved to do more. I studied to become a Licensed Professional Counselor Supervisor. Having the opportunity to offer counselor interns the same kind of quality training and learning experiences I had, satisfies the hunger.

While attending a business luncheon, shortly after going into private practice, we discussed our personal and professional backgrounds. When the age-old question of "Do you have children?" was posed, I shared my son had died. One colleague asked if my previous work in bereavement helped me through my grief journey. "It doesn't feel like it, but I'm sure it has," was the gist of my response.

Later that year, after learning I was developing a grief counseling guide, she deemed me an expert and requested a presentation for her interns specifically on bereavement therapy. After a year of such presentations and creating something I believed to be unique and necessary, I was encouraged (in large by others asking why I had not) to be compensated for my work. After much prayer, I received direction and the book title then started compiling my works.

The purpose of this book is twofold. It is meant to help mental health professionals provide quality, effective support to clients dealing with bereavement. It also offers pieces of my experiences in an artistic way to help people understand grief and inspire healing in grief. Readers will learn how to deal with the emotional, physical, social, and spiritual elements of grief.

NOTES

To Grievers

Thank you for taking another step on your grief journey. I understand how profound this walk can be and hope this guide will aid your path. This book focuses on bereavement, but the principals can apply to anything you are grieving. Some of the information provides guidelines to therapists. Feel free to read, skim, pass over, or use them personally. I recommend completing the activities and taking a week or so break between the chapters.

Taking time to settle into the concepts can be helpful. Rushing through the process can lead to emotional overwhelm. My personal experiences are meant to illustrate the topics. Many of our journeys contain distress, disappointment, and frustration. The stories and poems ("underbellies") I shared reflect mine, and some include strong language. Please safeguard yourself if needed. This book is designed to aid you on your journey or help you host a support group.

To Facilitators

Thank you for stepping up to the plate of grief counseling. You do not have to be afraid. Although it is going to take some preparation and work, I trust that you can provide quality, effective support to grieving clients. Preparing to facilitate a grief counseling or support group starts well before facilitating the group.

One of the first things to consider is whether your therapeutic orientation and personality align with what is needed to provide effective grief therapy. Grief is hard. Grief counselors need to have an essence of softness. If that is not your persona or skillset, please reconsider facilitating this group. The potential damage to participants that could result from harsh, rigidly structured facilitation is far too risky. If you discover that you are not emotionally capable of facilitating a grief group, seek your own professional treatment to resolve the issue(s) before moving forward.

Participants' experiences will likely impact you. It will be important that you are both professional and personable. Once you are set to continue, think about what you hope to accomplish with the group, then research and develop activities that will best support your goal(s). This guide is meant to offer you a framework. Explore your creativity to personalize your group.

You will find several of my poems ("underbellies") included in the guide as I believe they complement the topics. Like grief, some are raw and contain explicit verbiage. You are welcome to read and include them in your facilitation at your discretion.

Specifications for Helping Youth

Working with grieving youth is like working with grieving adults, but there are some differences. The delivery of the concepts below will need to be modified to be age appropriate for various groups. Children are concrete. They process the world more physically than adults. Therefore, turning the discussions into activities can make youth groups more effective.

When processing the warning signs of maladaptive bereavement, symptoms look different for adolescents as well. Unwarranted anger, self-harm, promiscuity, and school problems are pervasive with them. Youth are likely to disconnect and show no signs at all when the reality is unbearable.

Another note to consider is that children have less capacity to think abstractly. Thus, they may need less context and information than adults. Caregivers wondering what to share with them about the death should be encouraged to ask them what questions they have and answer honestly without unnecessary or gory details. The following is a list of phrases to avoid, the reasons why, and helpful alternatives.

Avoid: We lost "Grandma."

Rationale: They will want to find her. I mean, we do teach kiddos about finding lost things early on.

Replace with: "Grandma's" body stopped working. Her body is in the casket at the cemetery, but she is dead.

Avoid: "Sissy" is in a better place.

Rationale: They will want to go to the better place. Sibling competition does not necessarily end with death.

Replace with: "Sissy's" body stopped working. Her body is in the casket at the cemetery, but she is dead.

Avoid: "Grandpa" got very sick or went to sleep forever.

Rational: They will fear sickness and sleep. Who wants to do something that kills folks?

Replace with: "Grandpa" had cancer. The doctors/medicine helped him stay alive for as long as he could, but he is dead now.

Avoid: "Bubba" watches us when we sleep or is always looking over us.

Rationale: This might cause anxiety.

Replace with: We can always remember "Bubba." He is dead now, but we can love him forever.

Avoid: God needed "Auntie" to live with him.

Rationale: They may feel jaded that God did not want them to live with him or resent God for taking "Auntie."

Replace with: "Auntie's" body stopped working. Her body is in the casket at the cemetery, but she is dead. Her spirit is in heaven. Because we believe in God, our spirits will be with hers when we die.

Again, youth do not need an overload of information. Keeping spiritual/religious talk concrete and using the word dead can prevent confusion. If needed, use analogies of times when animals died for clarification.

Children are more adaptable and resilient than we think. Once their questions are answered, they will likely carry on with their regular scheduled programing. Refrain from projecting your grief expectations onto them.

As with adults, therapy is a great resource for complicated grief in adolescents. Lastly, children learn vicariously. Therefore, the most substantial thing caregivers can do to help grieving youth is to ensure that they themselves are grieving in the healthiest ways possible.

CHAPTER ONE

Opening

Before the Group

Develop your participation agreement and sign in sheet. If you need a starting point, ask fellow clinicians, and do some online research to identify what topics you want to include. Confidentiality and group guidelines are two of the basics. Identify which clients may be a good fit and extend the invite.

Collect the necessary materials which may include but are not limited to wooden cubes, sharpies, writing paper, writing utensils, construction paper, markers, sign in sheets, your group agreement, any supplemental reading excerpts, and any activity sheets you plan to use. If you are a spiritually based person, pray or meditate regarding the group and once you get the green light, have at it. It is helpful to remind members about the sessions. Grief brain can cause day and time confusion.

The Practicalities of the First Group Appointment

The objective of the initial meeting is to build rapport amongst the group. This is the foundation block, as members' willingness to be vulnerable is contingent upon feeling trust and connection. If this does not happen, participation will likely be minimal. The goal is to create a warm, inviting environment and give a thorough explanation of the group process. As a sign in sheet is going around, clearly introduce your qualifications. Discuss guidelines and have members sign the participation agreement. Regarding confidentiality, it is important to explain that the information and stories shared are likely to be some of the most intimate, private, meaningful information members own.

Therefore, members are free to share their personal information and experiences with loved ones, but not anything that could identify any other member. Explain that crying, laughter, anger, cursing, prayer, hugs/ touching, silence, fun, love, and talk of religion are to be expected. Some of these do not seem synonymous to grief, so explaining this may help alleviate confusion. Allow members to share their expectations.

Softly encourage everyone to share, but feel free to share as in depth or shallow as they please. Inform members that they are free to move at whichever rate they chose. I inform clients that there is no need to pressure themselves or others about how big or small the steps in their grief journeys are, because even pinky toe steps count.

Underbelly

"Sometimes Baby Steps Are Too Damn Big"

Pinky toe steps, because sometimes baby steps are too damn big

We've got to step up and play to win, but this grief game is rigged.

It's not even 1 step forward, 10 steps back. It's like all steps in the same place.

It doesn't matter if you step like an HBCU, a Goliath, a David, or a mouse. It's a lose-lose kinda race.

I applaud those who step out on faith.

They move with reckless hope in goodness and grace.

I applaud those who step in the name of love.

They move with forgiveness, vulnerability, kisses, and hugs.

I applaud those who step down when needed.

They move with humility and acceptance when they've been defeated.

I applaud those who step up to a challenge.

They move with confidence and bravery in balance.

These are toilsome steps to take!

Damn near impossible for Christ's sake!

"Take baby steps through hard situations," is what people tell.

But I know how big baby steps can be all too well.

After my baby stepped into my heart then took the stairways to heaven, I long jumped to hell.

And I've been trying to step out of Hades for so long, my feet have swelled.

Lao Tzu said, "the journey of a thousand miles begins with a single step,"

and Confucius said, "It doesn't matter how slow you go as long as you do not stop."

I encourage us to remember these proverbs when for the walk of life, we prep,

and allow me to step up and pile my own counselor's proverb on top.

Whether your plight is grief, insecurity, divorce, drugs, abuse or crossing any other bridge,

pinky toe steps, because sometimes baby steps are too damn big.

Opening circle

Each session starts with an opening circle activity. This sets the tone. It's like stretching before exercising; if we minimize its importance it can lead to unnecessary damage. In this case that looks like overwhelming or exposing members before they are comfortable. The following is the opening circle activity I facilitate until the group is closed (no more new members can join). It has proven to be powerful yet emotionally manageable as members first step into one another's experience instead of focusing on their own.

Thinking Outside the Box

- Pass out wooden cubes and sharpies.

- Suggest participants write something about their deceased person on each side of the cube (i.e. person's name, their age at death, a word that describes them, a favorite memory of them, their impact, etc.).

- Encourage participants to put their cubes in a box. This may be a difficult task for members as it may feel like they are giving their loved one away.

- Have everyone who is participating pick a cube out of the box that is not their own.

- Ask participants to write something, for example, a story/letter about, to, or from the deceased for the person whose cube they picked.

- Allow volunteers to read what they wrote.

- Suggest members give feedback amongst the group.

- Have participants return the cubes with the accompanying story/letter they wrote to the rightful owner.

- Explain the notion that we are here to share in and support each other's process, but not take them on as our own. This can help prevent members from experiencing vicarious grief.

The following is the opening circle activity I facilitate once the group is closed.

Stacked Up Collage

- Put out a piece of construction paper and markers.

- Encourage each member to put a word, phrase or picture related to their grief experience since the last session on the paper.

- Allow participants to explain and give feedback.

At all subsequent sessions, repeat the activity on the original piece of construction paper. At the end of the group members can see how their experiences stacked up. The following piece is an example of an entry for my personal opening circle activity.

Underbelly

"Dear Son in Heaven"

Peanut,

Eat your vegetables, listen to Jesus, clean up you toys, and don't forget to brush your teeth.

Infinity, Mom

Closing circle

Each session ends with a closing circle activity. This is a vital step because members may be emotionally spent. It is important to close the valve. Although, members are likely to continue to process the session on their own.

When working with adults, I usually allow for free will closing remarks, thoughts, feedback, and encouragers from members and facilitator(s). When working with children it may help to ask a direct question or have them select an item in the room that represents their session experience and share why.

Depending on participation there may be time left in the initial session. Facilitators can give a heads up about the topic for the next session, but I recommend wrapping the session up after that. Again, that first step may be as much as some can tolerate. Members might not give any indication but drop out can occur if they feel overwhelmed initially. Although I will not include opening and closing circles with each chapter, remember the benefit and necessity of opening and closing each meeting in an intentionally healthy way.

CHAPTER TWO

"Normal"

"Normal"

Some bereavement symptoms can feel so abnormal that individuals refrain from speaking out about them for fear of seeming "crazy." This leads to further maladaptive symptoms. The purpose here is to provide psychoeducation that promotes understanding and clarity, normalizes common symptomology, and informs about warning signs of unhealthy grief.

The idea that grief is like an ocean is gaining steam amongst grief specialist. Sometimes the waves brush gently across our feet, sometimes they shake us at the knees, and sometimes they suck us under. Even when we do not see or hear them, they are there. They never stop. Therefore, if we must be at the beach, we might as well learn to surf.

Everyone's journey is unique. Thus, there is no unanimous agreement on how grief is experienced. Even mental health professionals debate whether grief happens in stages, progresses through tasks, or is a compilation of common components that people experience. Kubler-Ross offers a stages theory and Grief Share operates from a components theory. I recommend you become familiar with and provide a brief explanation of the various perspectives. Allow members to share what resonates with them. Inform the group that there are other theories they can research as well. The following poem depicts my personal progression.

Underbelly

"The 7 D's of Death of Child"

Devastation

The moment you discover your child has died…It's like you get hit by a train, and then your remains get run through a shredder, but your brain doesn't die.

It's like you implode. And all that's left is a cloud of smoke and shards of what you used to be.

Drowning

After the initial blow,

you realize you've sunken to the lowest of lows.

Engulfed by the deepest and darkest blue,

convinced that not a single soul can see you

No air and little life,

no joy and tons of strife

with self, with God, with family and friends,

this is the closest thing to the end.

Desperation

Realizing you can't continue this way,

yearning to die, but fighting to stay

Begging God for a raft or vest,

promising to breathe if he'll do the rest

Silently crying out for help,

wishing you could trade the card you were dealt

Divine intervention

The space between suicide and living, where something bigger than you is preventing the former and permitting the later.

Surviving off the prayers of the righteous and the Holy Spirit himself; one day you realize you're stronger, yet sadder.

Dreaming

Fantasizing about the future; seeing yourself healed and happy

or at least less zombie

considering another child for the first time.

Pictures of names, genders, and faces fleet by.

Doubt

Questioning everything you've ever believed

Posing questions like "how come God never has to say I'm sorry" and "does God cry for me." Finding it impractical to have faith in something you can't see

and outlandish to believe one day you'll feel relief

Day to Day

Realizing that life from now on is just picking up enough shards to be alive enough to move.

Not on, but to the next piece.

And then one day, we hope, we'll have collected enough pieces to be some kind of being again. A being that can smile, love, laugh, hope, and believe

or at least bear

I pray to see y'all there.

Angel parents, I'm so sorry we're a thing, and my heart is with us.

Grief does not follow a specific set of rules. Because of this, grief expectations can cause guilt and lead to anxiety. Ask members to write and share the grief expectations they have of themselves and others and the ones they believe others have for them. Have participants choose which expectations they want to discard and which ones they want to reframe and work towards. Encourage members to help each other transform their expectations into affirmations that are reasonable, attainable, and hopeful.

At the beginning of my journey, I felt pressure to be grateful for the time we got to spend with Peanut and the potential opportunity of mothering another earth residing child in the future. However, there was no gratitude in my reality. Addressing my guilt freed me to take more steps on my path.

Underbelly

"Fuck this Club"

Fuck this club.

The "Angel Mom's Club" that is

The club that people keep telling me God hand picks the strongest moms for membership

The club where the only eligibility requirement, is that you lost the one damn thing that made you eligible in the first place

The club where ladies get in free, but we pay for the rest of our lives with pieces of our souls

The club where instead of "turn down for what?"

it's more like "get out of bed for what?

Be grateful for what?

Wash my ass for what?"

The club where we wear sad eyes instead of makeup,

chase our antidepressants with wine,

and have sleepless nights instead of one-night stands

People keep telling me it's an honor to be a part of this club.

Fuck this club.

Being a part of this club won't change the fact that my child is dead.

So, fuck this club.

Being a part of this club doesn't make me less depressed or make me cry any less.

So, fuck this club.

Being a part of this club doesn't help me decide whether to say I have a son, or I had a son.

So, fuck this club.

Being a part of this club doesn't make Mother's Day, Halloween, Thanksgiving, (my son was born on Thanksgiving),

or Christmas any less excruciating.

So, fuck this club.

Being a part of this club won't erase the images of my baby

laying cold,

stiff,

and lifeless in a casket.

So, fuck this club.

Being a part of this club doesn't change the fact that I will never see my son walk,

or hear him talk

or see him ride a bike, or eat ice cream, or go to prom, or graduate.

So, fuck this club.

People keep telling me,

"God must've known you could handle it."

Man, fuck Gaaaaaahhh.

No.

I can't go that far.

That's not the name of this piece.

I mean,

I'm a good Christian woman.

I was raised in the church.

I sang in the choir.

I go to bible study and give my tithes.

I know that "God is good all the time, and all the time God is good."

So, I can't say fuck God, right?

So here I am.

Member of the "Angel Moms' Club"

Avoiding sad songs and babies

Losing weight

Praying each night that I won't wake up

Pretending like I'm ok so that others feel comfortable

Getting back to "normal" and going back to work 3 months after Peanut's death

'Cause that's enough time, right?

Dancing solo to the sound of survivor's guilt that's loud enough to bust my eardrums

Suffering in silence until God answers my prayers

Sporting my angel mom badge

As if I'm not screaming on the inside

FUCK THIS CLUB!

All grief experiences are normal, although some are not healthy. It is common for people to grieve in unhealthy ways. Have clients reflect on their symptoms and the symptoms of their loved ones. Encourage members to speak up and seek help if they notice unhealthy grief. Discuss healthy coping skills like crying, talking, art, spiritual practices, physical wellness activities, having fun, laughing, engaging in meaningful work and projects, and seeking professional help.

The possible physical impacts of grief are enormous. These may include loss or increase of appetite with accompanying weight changes, sleeplessness, loss of memory, anxiety, headaches, and stomach aches. Encourage members to seek help if these symptoms prevent functioning. Read the "How You Get Unstuck" excerpt from Tiny Beautiful Things. The following is the story of my experience with the physical ramifications of bereavement.

Underbelly

"X-Men: The Inside Out Girl Story"

My brain scrambled when the nurse confirmed Peanut was dead.

The bolt of horror zapped me from 29 to my death bed.

I woke up and thought "oh, so this is it."

The world was a spin top.

I was staggering. I dropped my cup. My speech was weird. I couldn't fasten my shoe buckles due to a Parkinson's like tremor.

I was not drunk.

I was deeply perplexed.

I had heard that 30 came with challenges digesting beef and minor aches and pains, but I missed the memo on this stuff.

My mom threatened to move in with me if I didn't go see a doctor, and my supervisor threatened to call my mom if I didn't go see a doctor. So, I saw a doctor.

He stuck a 9-inch needle into my spine and drained out a liter of fluid (that I'm convinced was never supposed to leave my body). Then he informed me I had Multiple Sclerosis, the autoimmune condition that attacks the nervous system.

Damn.

People had literally gotten on my last nerve.

Physical and emotional bones fractured from the news, but I was determined to live my normal life. I planned to adhere to the suggestions regarding eating and life- style choices that were aimed at slowing the deterioration of my nervous system.

The most stressed suggestion, pun intended, was managing stress in healthy ways. So, I got serious about yoga, reeled way back on fried food, and ramped up my poetry writing.

That summer I developed the coping skill of pulling weeds from my yard.

I'd long for it throughout the day then pull till my hands cramped.

It was a great stress reliever. But, one afternoon as the Texas heat raged, I got dizzy again.

This time it was more like on the mirror ride at a carnival dizzy than world spinning dizzy.

My teenage nephew noticed my bout and brought me some water and a chair.

I slouched and sprawled while vacuuming in air for a bit.

I didn't drop my cup or experience any other symptoms, so I got back to it.

The next day, as if my nerves were on top of my skin, I could feel everything!

I could feel each fiber of my clothes, the wind inside my bones, and the ground through my shoes.

My nephew said "You're like a superhero. We should call you Inside Out Girl."

I didn't feel super or like a hero.

I just felt like a mutant.

The name fit, so I came up with the tag line "she wears her heart on her sleeve and her brain on her pantleg."

I have been living my kind of normal life. I'm a counselor. I drive. I still do yoga and poetry, and I've not been hospitalized since being diagnosed.

I conquered the weed pulling obsession, but sometimes I still spontaneously combust.

Too much stress and here comes a torch down my legs and feet.

I'm learning to accept it though.

Afterall I always loved the X-Men, and I can't deny the similarities we share.

We live normal-ish lives until high stress situations pull our insides out.

One of these days I'm going to get a nervous system body suit made and submit my application to Professor X.

CHAPTER THREE

Dealing and More Dealing

Dealing

Dealing with grief is taxing, so some avoid it. This is understandable but may lead to more challenges. The purpose here is to provide a guideline for journeying through grief in a healthy way.

Although depression is a common effect of grief, it is not healthy. Signs to look for include but are not limited to contemplating suicide, withdrawal, sleep problems, alcohol/drug use, eating problems, memory loss, anger, and physical issues. Encourage members to speak up and seek help if any of these symptoms impede their functioning. Reaching out to a loved one or acquaintance is a healthy first step. They can support you in seeing a doctor, counselor/therapist, and finding support groups. The following poem details what depression looked like for me in the beginning of my journey.

Underbelly

"Year Two"

Free falling

From nowhere to nowhere else

Traveling in place

Yearning for purpose and belonging, and becoming one with the void

It's suitable here, I guess.

It's not stopping on the train tracks or flask in my purse.

It's waking up and showering at least.

It's full here.

Of loneliness, grief, despair, but it's full at least

There's room here too.

For possibilities

And sometimes others stop by.

They leave, but it's nice to see them.

The feelings are unwavering, and the tears still flow, but they're separated by more seconds than before and that helps.

I think.

I held a baby in year two.

Yeah, it was as beautiful and destructive as I feared it would be.

I miss how my brain protected me from taking in the reality of life in year one.

Sometimes I could really use a dose of that shock.

I look forward to year 3 and 12 and 38.

Maybe I won't remember how your hair smelled, or how you used to scratch my neck when I held you upright.

I look forward to year 4ish or 6 or something. Maybe I'll get another shot.

And although your spot can never be filled, I can finally hope that another baby might do something for me.

Any damn thing

Year two has been one hell of a year.

I gave myself a Mother's Day present from you.

Multiple Sclerosis…aka "the stressing disease"

And although I believe you want me to be happy; in a warped way, I feel like this "gift" is proof that I love you so much it'll always hurt.

I put up a picture of you in the hallway and took some of your stuff out of the boxes.

I barricaded it behind some heavy storage bins, but sometimes I'm strong enough to go in there.

I almost had a birthday party for you.

I couldn't quite go through with it, but I'm rooting for next year.

Most people have moved on with their lives.

The calls and texts have stopped, and your dad got married and has another baby on the way.

Your Grandma Linda is still here though.

Sometimes the pain in her eyes is too much to bear, but I'm happy I'm not here alone.

I still can't listen to Sade's "Sweetest Gift" or Beyoncé's "Blue," but Lauryn's "To Zion" played once while I was in the shower, and I made it through virtually unscathed.

That's progress, right?

Year two's brought a little sleep relief,

and ambulances and hospitals are becoming bearable again.

I hear time heals all wounds, and I sure hope that's true.

At this point, I'd count every second if it'll even remotely help me through.

They say, "joy comes in the morning," but they never tell you which one.

It didn't come in the 1st year, and year two's almost done.

But I haven't given up. I'm gonna hang in there if it's the only thing I do.

So, rest assured my angel prince, my love for you is carrying me through year two.

Family, friends, coworkers, and strangers often mean well. They do not always do well. Once I told a grieving loved one whose brother had died that she could borrow mine. She didn't whack me and accepted my apology for the ill-timed, subpar (though good-natured) offer. But every time I recall how unintentionally insensitive that was, I cringe. We can minimize conflict by being honest and giving grace. Other people are grieving our loved one(s) with us, and each person may do that in a different way. Some people will have no idea we are grieving; therefore, they may not know that we are sensitive to certain things. Read "The Black Arc of It" from Tiny Beautiful Things. Because grief *is* like an ocean, it is fitting to facilitate the Life Savers activity here. Afterwards share the "Technical Foul" story which details an incident of me dealing with a stranger.

Life Savers

- Ensure each member has writing utensils and a copy of the Life Savers handout provided in the resource section of this book.

- Share the concept that it is nearly impossible to save oneself from drowning, literally and in grief. We often need other people, places, and things to help us.

- Have members identify and write on the buoy who and what helps them deal with grief.

- Allow for discussion.

Alternative Activities:

Sensational Survival Kits

- Hand out paper and writing utensils.

- Share the idea that our 5 senses can help ground us in the overwhelming moments of grief.

- Have members identify and write things they can keep in a kit to help cope when overwhelmed.

- Encourage them to include items they can see, touch, taste, smell and hear.

Some examples may include a picture of the deceased or a vacation spot, a stress ball, a piece of gum or peppermint, an essential oil, and a favorite song.

Recipes for Relief

This activity follows the same concept and structure of the Life Savers activity, but members write their "helpers" as a recipe instead of on a buoy. A template is provided in the resource section of this book.

Underbelly

Technical Foul

Peanut had been dead almost a year. At a feeble 92 pounds, I was slipping in and out of consciousness. I went in for an MRI. A smooth faced, bright eyed tech greeted me with "oh my goodness, you're so skinny! How do you stay so small?"

Fighting back an eye roll, I took a deep breath, and exhaled "grief."

As if I were speaking Pig Latin, his nose crinkled under his pointed brows and his chin tilted to the side.

"My son died," I clarified.

From his flushed, volcanic face oozed "I am so sorry and so stupid. I can't even imagine!"

"Please don't try to, the images will kill your appetite," I jabbed.

He dropped his head, teary eyed, and clenched my manila chart so tight it crumpled beneath the pressure. He scurried to the MRI machine.

I trust that he will be more mindful and sensitive when talking to others about their weight now that he understands that grief can be a factor.

Underbelly

"Rainbows aren't Supposed to Make You Cry, and Lions aren't Supposed to Make You Want to Die"

Rainbows aren't supposed to make you cry, and lions aren't supposed to make you want to die. But both of those things happen with me and here's why:

Double rainbows

The first time I ever saw a double rainbow, I was 7 weeks pregnant.

I had recently discovered that my live-in hubby researched how to use Naproxen to cause me to have a miscarriage.

He had been cheating, and he had just lost his job, so he was out of town working with family while we caught our bearings.

Heartbroken, irate, and ready to commit a murder-suicide,

I was a six-car pileup!

My OBGYN told me that I had to try not to stress because my baby could feel everything I felt. To alleviate the trepidation of him executing his intention, my mom and I packed up his stuff and started on our way to drop it off to him.

It was a partly sunny and warm day, but it was raining off and on.

My mom insisted that she drive.

She was concerned I was too emotional to focus.

She can be a worry-bot and an over-doer, but she was right.

I couldn't focus on anything other than having a complete breakdown and stressing my baby to death.

To distract myself, I gazed out the window.

We were on a toll road behind Austin, TX.

Watching snails crawl would've been less boring.

There wasn't anything out there but a few boars and some crop fields.

The sky showcased a thick, bright rainbow and a thin, faint rainbow behind it.

I thought "wow it's like my baby and I in the midst of the storm."

Tears of joy drizzled down my cheeks.

The second time I saw a double rainbow I was 5 1/2 months pregnant.

I had gone into preterm labor and was hospital confined for the rest of my pregnancy.

I was stir-crazy.

A few days in and outside was still off limits.

Eat times were spaced like planets.

Showers were cancelled and nurse assistance was mandatory for getting out of bed to pee.

The crisis alerts of the patients in the rooms surrounding me echoed all day and night.

I envisioned myself running out of the building with my gown flapping showing my cheeks, like in the movies.

God must've known I was close to the edge because someone opened the blinds for me right before I made a dash for it.

It had been raining, and the sky showcased another rainbow with a faint sidekick.

I thought "wow it's really Peanut (we'd already given him a nickname) and me in the midst of the storm."

I cried tears of hope.

The third time I saw a double rainbow was a few months after Peanut died.

Forgive my lack of detail about this one.

The first 8 months are blurry.

A few things are sketched into my memory though.

1. This double rainbow was positioned straight up and down. I didn't even know rainbows could do that!

2. Grief strangled me so bad a waterfall burst from my eyes.

3. This time I thought, "God please make it stop! If I never see another double rainbow again it'll be too soon!"

I've yet to see another.

Lions

One of my two favorite movies is The Lion King.

I know everyone likes The Lion King,

but if it were legal, I'd marry The Lion King.

Like, to this day I quote it in daily conversation.

So naturally, Peanut's theme was "prince of the jungle."

My mom decked his room out!

He had jungle: bed set, rugs, stuffed animals, pictures, curtains, and the music thing that dangles over the crib (forgive me I didn't learn what those are called).

After Peanut died, my mom started collecting lions.

She doesn't do anything small.

She had a vast collection.

Every now and then, she'd gift me one.

Every one of them hit like a window shield to a moth.

A reminder of the death loss I couldn't forget.

I didn't tell her because I didn't want to make her feel bad.

She was trying to help, why make her sad?

Then she brought me a shoe box full of lion figurines.

I just couldn't!

I disintegrated.

She apologized emphatically.

Saying she didn't mean to upset me.

It's just that lions help her feel close to Peanut and she hoped they'd make me happy.

I poured, "lions don't make me happy; they make me wanna die."

I've not gotten anymore.

I know this isn't customary, but I've got a favor to ask of everyone that hears this piece.

If you ever see a double rainbow or lion, lift this prayer up with me.

"Lord we're gathered here today, on behalf of the gal with the heavenly lion prince boy.

God please mend her heart and restore her joy.

Hear her needs through her heavy sighs

And let her rest in your comfort that rainbows won't always make her cry and lions won't always make her want to die.

Amen"

More Dealing

Guilt is common, but it is often detrimental. It can lead to feeling stuck and even depression. People tend to avoid addressing situations in which they feel they have done wrong because of shame and embarrassment. Inspiration is far more powerful and effective in motivating folks to address those situations and feelings.

Have members reflect on their old and new expectations and encourage them to "throw your *shoulds* away." Address and normalize survivor's guilt. I have found that parents, spouses, and siblings have particular struggles with survivor's guilt because of the perceived relational responsibilities. Read "The Obliterated Place" from Tiny Beautiful Things.

Death loss can lead to us blaming the deceased or others. Sometimes people's actions are linked to the death and sometimes we just need to place responsibility somewhere. Unforgiveness can impede healing by damaging relationships with self, the deceased, others, and God. Forgiveness can be freeing and can lead to mending those support relationships, but it can be challenging. I have identified 8 common components of forgiveness. They are:

- the incident (someone hurt another's feelings or made them mad)
- the desire to let go of anger/resentment or be free of guilt
- addressing the incident with or without the person(s) depending on whether it is feasible
- verbalizing an apology or forgiveness stance
- change of behavior or relationship dynamic if the behavior does not change
- change in the vibe of the relationship (negative feelings subside)
- removal of the incident from conversation and conscious (it is not talked or thought about)
- removal of any residual effects of the incident (i.e. it is no longer driving current actions)

Discuss these components and urge clients to work on forgiving those they blame or resent for the death loss.

Again, family, friends, coworkers, and strangers often mean well. They do not always do well. This subtopic is substantial. It can be helpful to allow more time for it before moving on. Sometimes we scramble along our journeys. To appease each other we, may spew out myths, love lies (lies we tell people to keep from hurting their feelings), and other stupid stuff. Have members write and share the unhelpful things people have said/done. Share my "Oh No Nat…It's Time" story.

Underbelly

"Oh No Nat…It's time." A Story of unhelpful advice and forgiveness

To honor Peanut's first "angelversary", I made a memorial of his clothes, stuffed animals, and books in a closet. I used to go in there and sniff his stuff and snot cry reading "The Tawny Scrawny Lion."

My good friend, the mother of two little dumplings that would melt an iceberg's heart, called to check on me. I shared what I had done with Peanut's belongings.

"Oh no Nat, you've got to get rid of that stuff! It's time! Keeping that is just going to make it worse!"

Easy for her to say! She had her sons that she got to touch every day! How dare she tell me to get rid of the only remnants of Peanut that I could still touch?

I mulled then remembered that she was my closest friend. We had been helping and supporting one another for years. Neither wanted to see the other hurt.

She cut me, but I knew her intention was to bandage. Therefore, in my mind, I reframed what she said.

"Oh Nat, that's such a crippling scene to imagine. I bet you wail and are shattered when you're in there. I wish I could unbreak your heart. I can't imagine my sons dying. Maybe getting rid of those reminders would help."

I don't think anything could have made me feel better but hearing her message this way helped me forgive her. We never had to speak about it again.

Dealing with ourselves can be one of the most difficult parts of the grief journey. We tend to be so tough on ourselves which makes the journey much harder than it already is. Review reasonable and attainable affirmations, then have members develop at least one to self-encourage.

Underbelly

"One Day I'm gonna Write a Happy Piece"

One day I'm gonna write a happy piece.

It's going to be about love and joy and butterflies and bubbles.

But today is not that day.

Today I'm going to write about grief.

Again

About how on my journey I've learned you can both sink and swim

About how I both love my son to life and wish I could forget him

About how just when I think I'm healing, grief seeps through my scabbed skin

About how I'm now convinced the yellow brick road is a metaphor for grief… because I can't get over, I can't get out of the game and I sure can't win

One day I'm gonna write a happy piece.

It's going to be about marriage and kids and cupcakes and cookies.

But today is not that day.

Today I'm going to write about faith.

About how on my journey I've learned you can both pray and stray

About how weeping often endures through the nights and hangs around through the days

About how I don't care what God's reason was, I wanted you to stay

About how God's presence and yours feel like one in the same

The more I yearn to hold them close the more they seem to fade.

One day I'm gonna write a happy piece.

It's going to be about wealth and beaches and family and fun.

But today is not that day.

Today I'm going to write about hope.

About how it's both keeping me alive and killing me too

About how I hope you remember me as much as I remember you

About how I hope I'll still get to teach you how to read, write and tie your shoes

About the letter that I wrote to Hope that just reads "I'm sorry, but we're through"

I promise, one day I'm gonna write a happy piece.

It's going to be about healing and cotton candy and friends and forgiveness.

But today is just not that day.

CHAPTER FOUR

Recap & Not Grief

Recap

We have learned and processed a great deal so far. Refresh and take a breather. If the group were an open group this is where I recommend capping entry. At this point, new members would have missed the essential foundation of the group and it would be challenging to cultivate cohesion. With so much information some, important concepts may have been forgotten. It can be helpful to provide a brief review of the previous topics and allow for any input or questions.

Not Grief

Other life stressors/happenings can exacerbate or distract us from grief. Two things can be true at once. We can have grief and joy. We can have both grief and fun. This section is meant to allow for a step outside of grief. Have participants write and share their "not grief" stuff. "Sometimes I Wanna Punch my Dog" is an example of mine. Remind members that they have learned how to deal with grief, and they can apply what they learned to these situations.

Now for some fun! Laughter and joy produce chemicals in the brain that fight the chemicals produced by depression. Play a board game or do an enjoyable physical activity. Those healing chemicals are sure to generate here! Some games that are entertaining, and open communication are Scategories, Pictionary, Taboo, and Gestures.

"Sometimes I Wanna Punch my Dog"

Sometimes I wanna punch my dog.

Not to hurt him of course

But the whimpering when I'm too tired to play really works my nerves.

Like, doesn't he know it's a constant reminder that I'm not enough?

Not trustworthy enough for God to let me keep my son

Not valuable enough for my own husband to treat me like I'm the one

Not loved enough for family and friends to keep their word

And not even fun enough to keep a dog from being bored

Man, sometimes I really wanna punch my dog.

Like when he disregards the sensitivity of my feet and shins

Or when I tell him to go to bed and, in dog language, he calls me a bi**h

Like, why doesn't he care about my body or my feelings at all?

And here I am buying him jerseys and boots from the mall.

I know I shouldn't, but sometimes I truly wanna punch my dog.

Like when his hair is all over my clothes in public

And when he incessantly sniffs and licks other dogs "pubics"

Seriously, doesn't he understand how embarrassing that is?

Got people thinking "no home training" is how we live.

Y'all I love him dearly, but sometimes I wanna punch my dog.

CHAPTER FIVE

Grief and God

Grief and God

With depression and suicidal ideation being common elements of grief, having a sense of connection to a source outside of self can create the hope needed to carry on. Be mindful that individuals will likely vary in spiritual subscriptions. I chose the word God because I knew it resonated with each member. Feel free to use a word like divinity or something else if it fits better. The purpose here is to provide a safe space to discuss the fact that spirituality and religion, or the lack thereof, can play a major role in the bereavement process. For some it may be sustaining. It can be a source of pain or strife for others. Yet, there are those who will find it irrelevant. Encourage inclusion of all belief systems. Facilitate an open discussion on the role of spirituality and religion in grief.

Grief can lead individuals to question their beliefs. Have members write and share any questions they have. Bereavement can lead to anger, disappointment, and disconnection. Normalize these feelings and, encourage clients to authentically express them. Holding them in can lead to more complications. I always say, "Anger is like farts. Better out than in, but in appropriate spaces." Healthy ways to process negative emotions include writing and high impact physical activities. It is my opinion that God can handle our true feelings. I do not believe the all-knowing and all-powerful needs us to lie or stifle ourselves. Writing "God Must've Sneezed" was the authentic expression of my death loss experience. Emphasize the value and magnitude of hope. Reiterate that positive emotions produce chemicals in the body that counteract the chemicals depression produces.

Underbelly

"God Must've Sneezed"

They say God will never leave nor forsake you. So, he must've just sneezed.

'Cause I prayed so hard for him to protect my son, that I bruised up both my knees.

So, it had to be an accident. They say you must close your eyes to sneeze.

That must be why he didn't hear my pregnant hospital cry of "Jesus pleeeease.

If he must go, take him now. Don't let me meet him if he has to leave."

Good parents listen to their children and take their desires to heart.

So, I refuse to believe God our Father decided that "death of baby" was how my motherhood should start.

You cannot sneeze with your eyes open.

So, here's what I'm hoping:

That at about 6:00 am on Wednesday March 25th, 2015

God noticed my Peanut struggling to breathe.

He jumped up and rushed to his bed

But a sneeze caught him mid grab.

"Hachew!"

And by the time he opened his eyes Peanut was blue.

I mean, God was human once before.

Maybe he took sneezing with him back behind Heaven's doors.

Yeah, that must be it.

This is the only version in which I can sit.

The only thing I can believe

Is that he didn't sign off on Peanut's death. God must've sneezed.

It can be challenging to feel a divine presence after bereavement. Some will find comfort in scripture or other writings. Have members share what passages/encouragers have helped them along their journeys.

Underbelly

"Ole School Miracle"

I wish God were still in the business of performing ole school miracles.

Don't get me wrong.

I think new jobs, and getting out of tickets, and rainbows are cool.

But I'm in need of an ole school miracle.

I don't want to sound ungrateful.

I appreciate my house, car, family, and friends.

But I'm in need of an ole school miracle.

Really.

Female intuition has been miraculous to me.

I've seen people walk away from car accidents that should've been fatal.

I know people who've won their wars with cancer.

And Santonio Holmes' Super Bowl 43 catch was UN-real.

But I'm in need of an ole school miracle.

Now I'll admit, it may be that I'm not praying "good enough."

So, God can't hear my cries.

But I need a miracle like in 2nd Kings when God used Elisha to take the Shamanite's son from lying dead on the couch to sneezing and opening his eyes.

I'll tell the truth.

I've said a few curse words in my day. I've tossed a few back, and even had a child out of wedlock.

So, I know I need a miracle like no other.

Like in Luke when God had compassion on the woman from Nain who lost her only son by touching his coffin and returning him to his mother.

I confess.

I stayed in bed a few times when I should've been in God's house.

So, I know I'm not deserving to even fix my mouth!

That's why I know I need an ole school miracle.

Like in 1st Kings when that widow brought her dead son to Elijah all hysterical

I imagine, like me, she was too broken to go to God on her own

and needed a friend to intercede for God to bring life back to his bones.

But when I think about it, I might already have the ole school miracle I really need.

Because I don't know how I could be surviving my grief

Unless like he promised in Philippians 4, God has given me peace beyond all understanding.

During this session of my group, God was labeled silent, absent, distant, disappointing, and scary. Both sorrow and hope filled me. I was sorrowful that each of those resonated with me and felt responsible to be a beacon of hope. Amid pondering how to balance the two, the Holy Spirit reminded me that the one thing The Word equates God with is love (1 John 4:8). I shared that and encouraged participants to list their physical representations of love. It was monumental. I urge you to have your group do the same.

Underbelly

"Love ICU"

This piece was inspired by a conversation I had with a friend who was in a thrilling new relationship. She described her beaux as her "love doctor" sharing that she'd never experienced a love so nurturing. We reflected on my life and joked that I needed a "love hospital." After the events surrounding Peanut's death (including the dissolution of most of my friendships and "familyships"), I needed a Love Intensive Care Unit (ICU). Submersed in so much pain, it took years for me to feel or see the love that was surrounding me, but here they are.

Mom

My earth angel

The one God uses to keep me from throwing in the towel

The one who decorates his site and visits Peanut even now

The one who travels to the bottom of the ocean with me

The one who understands my grief journey will take time and just lets it be

Love I see you.

Veronica

The one who searched through Peanut's clothes to find a bib I was looking for

The one who left my first Mother's Day card at my front door

The one who journeyed with me back to Peanut's NICU

Love I see you.

Music

Specifically Cranes in the Sky, The Thrill of it All, Give You Blue, Inspired by True Events and Gospel

The one I blast throughout my home

The one who convinces me I'm not alone

The one who sees my ugliest cries

The one who gets me to dance when I feel I could die

Love I see you.

Brit Brat and Nik

The ones who opened their homes to me when mine was eating me alive

The ones who acknowledged him from their tribe

Love I see you.

Bryan-Andrew

The one who became a lion to honor my boy

The one who took it as his personal duty to revive my joy

Love I see you.

Ebony

My childhood bestie

The one who validated me as a mother by crying "he was real"

The one who was kind enough to gift me her friends to help me heal

Love I see you.

Poetry and Fusha's Lounge

My sanctuary

The one who makes me brave when I am scary

The one who never makes me feel judged

The one who sees the entirety of my insides and gives me snaps and hugs

Love I see you.

Sho, Jonnie, Megan, and Jen

The ones who are my friends

The ones whose prayer and humor carry me when I feel I'm at the end

Love I see you.

Ryan fam

The ones who sent me a life raft when a grief wave sucked me under

The ones I know are there without a thought or wonder

Love I see you.

Jonathan

The one who didn't pander to my pain

The one who convinced me that if I let go of grief, I could be refilled with love amidst the rain

Love I see you.

Pastor Brown

My Messenger

The one who speaks life into my lungs

The one who reminds me I always have the lord when I feel I have no one

Love I see you.

Rocco

My dog son

The one who fills the void

The one who sees me crying and brings me toys

Love I see you.

Nicole aka Nikki boo

The one who gifted him his home going shoes

Love I see you.

Clients

"Good Griefers" and more

The ones who make me believe I still have some purpose in store

Love I see you.

Mrs. Edna

The one who cared about me the person more than me the employee

The one who forced me to take care of me

Love I see you.

Page fam

The ones who traveled cross country to honor Peanut twice

The ones who showed up no matter the distance, attendees, or price

Love I see you.

Mama Debbie, Aunt Tese, and Will

The ones who entered my life well after Peanut was gone

But honored him like they knew him all along

Love I see you.

Uncle Ray and his clan

The ones who matched me in broadcasting my little man

Love I see you.

Bill

The one who blessed Peanut's life when I could not

The one who made sure he went home like a big shot

Love I see you.

Uncle Dene

The one whose love is practical in nature

The one who picks up the slack and carried Peanut to meet his maker

Love I see you.

Foreign Missions and Women's Ministries

The ones who made me feel alive

The ones claimed my victory when I thought I'd die

Love I see you.

Teedie & Baby J

The ones who show gratitude no matter how far away

The ones who it doesn't matter how long it been since we've been in touch

They've assured me they love Peanut and me so much

Love I see you.

Aunt Kim

The one whose support is always in the background

The one who dressed Peanut to go in the ground

Love I see you.

Deleen and Paula

My old school homies

The ones who said we'd always be bros and pulled up to his wake to show me

Love I see you.

Dad

The one who pinky promises it will be ok

The one who I know sends up a prayer for me every single day

Love I see you.

Mrs. Cannon

The one who unfortunately knows how I feel

The one who when I asked if it gets easier kept it real

Love I see you.

Uncle Matt

The one who used his voice to MC Peanut's ceremony

The one who comforts my comforter when she's lonely

Love I see you.

Holy Spirit

The one who saw me stopping on the tracks and responded

The one who keeps Peanut and I bonded

Love I see you.

Peanut

My baby boy

My pride and joy

The one that became my heart, broke it, and saves it every day

The one I miss within each fiber of my being and in every single way

Love I see you.

And last but not least-est,

everyone else who's prayed for me, wished me well, or snapped to my grief pieces

Love I see you.

CHAPTER SIX

Commemorating

Commemorating

Deciding how to relate to the deceased and what to do with their belongings can be a daunting task. The purpose here is to destigmatize and normalize how members choose to connect with the dead. There is no right or wrong way to commemorate the deceased.

Offer encouragement regarding deciding what to do with their person's belongings without judgement. Urge members to trust their timing. Encourage them to do what they need to do in balance with what they can do (i.e. sell the person's belongings). Remind members to lean on others when they find that they are unable to complete necessary tasks. Many people are eager to help. They may not have an idea of how to do so, thus, giving them options can be helpful.

Grievers might feel pressure regarding making "shrines." That force can be minimized through assurance that memorials can be public, private or in our hearts. Allow members to share what they have done, are struggling to do, and have decided not to do on their journeys. Share "You Washed Away Peanut."

Underbelly

"You Washed Away Peanut"

Even after 3 years, Peanut's comforter set was still on the bed in his memorial room. It had some of his baby goo residue on it which helped me feel connected to him physically. One weekend, my nephew B had a couple of friends stay the night. Because there were other guest rooms, I didn't expect anyone to trespass in Peanut's. However, in true entitled teenage fashion, B decided that his room with a queen-sized bed wasn't big enough for him and his pals. Unbeknownst to me, he spread them out hotel style, giving them each their own room. A few days later, while spending time in Peanut's memorial, I noticed the comforter looked fuzzy. It was a unique suede material, so it was easy to see that something was different. Peering closer, I realized Peanut's goo was gone! A *shrilling* yelp escaped me. It almost felt like he had died… again. One minute he was here and the next he was gone. I must've scared B. Normally he sloths when he hears my voice, but this time he zipped over. Frantically, I asked him if he knew what happened to the comforter. Obliviously, he shared that he washed it after his friend slept on it, because "he knows how I am." With an airless groan, as if punched in the gut, came *"PEANUT'S DNA WAS ON THERE; YOU WASHED AWAY PEANUT!"* As if he saw a ghost, his rich cocoa frame morphed into dark sapphire stone. He exclaimed "I'm so sorry Aunt Nat, I had no idea!" I don't remember what happened afterwards, but sometime later I realized another reframe was needed. Peanut was not that comforter or any of his other belongings. Truth is, I had no control over what might happen to his stuff. In North Texas, a tornado could wipe out everything in the blink of an eye. If I wanted Peanut's essence to live on, I had to find another way. Because Peanut was a resource of so much love, I decided to keep his essence alive by purposefully loving myself and others. As for B, it was clear he did not intend to destroy my cherished blanket. I mustered up every grain of grace and mercy possible to work on forgiving him. I believe he learned a valuable lesson about respecting boundaries that he will carry with him in the future.

Holidays, birthdays, and "anniversaries" can be brutal. Again, offer encouragement regarding decisions on how to navigate traditions/rituals or not. Permissions can help alleviate guilt and supports can help carry the heaviness these dates may bring. Have members write and share personal permissions and advise them to have supports in place for these dates.

Underbelly

"I Haven't"

I haven't written a grief piece in a while.

I haven't been depressed or crying as much, though it's still hard to smile.

I feel kind of guilty.

But I ain't mad at the lil break because whew chile,

for a minute there, I was grieving like grief was going out of style.

In my shoes, most can't take a step let alone walk a mile.

And I wouldn't even recommend they try 'cause this buried my only child 'ish; this shit is wild.

I haven't been praying much lately. Guess I don't know what else to say.

I haven't even been thinking about praying before at night I lay.

I feel like God must know what it means when he sees my heart and soul decay.

And if he sees fit to intervene, I suppose he just may.

My pain, most won't ever face.

And I'm glad only a few unfortunates will ever have to live in this coffin like space.

I wouldn't even wish that on the devil, whom I hate.

I haven't been to his gravesite since laying him there.

I haven't sent a flower nor a stuffed bear.

I feel like people must understand that although I'm usually *Supa* tough, when it comes to that, I'm hella scared.

My struggle, most seem to genuinely care.

And I appreciate those who have always been here.

I wouldn't be making it through this journey that ain't no type-a fair

without them lifting prayers, cups, and smoke for me in the air.

As we learn and decide to transfer the love we have for the deceased into more abstract concepts, it can be healing to create things that symbolize our journeys. Assign homework of members starting to make a tangible "Love Creation" to share or not in an upcoming session. This can be a letter, song, poem, painting, or any other expression. It does not necessarily need to be made by the individual.

Underbelly

"N.A.T.H.A.N.I.E.L. L.E.E."

N: for the nights I spend tossing and turning

Stomach churning, brain burning and soul a yearning

A: for the agony, my body can't overcome

The heartbreak and despair rolled tightly into one

T: for the tears I just can't control

The more I fight to hold them back the heavier they flow.

H: for Heaven; oh, how I pray to meet you there.

You, Me, Grandma, and Jesus what a family affair.

A: for alone; I guess this is my new normal.

All by myself rolling 'round in the turmoil

N: for never, and this is a fact

I'll never stop missing you, and you're never coming back.

I: for infinity, remember that was our word?

I'd say I love you with my finger without ever being heard.

E: for the eagerness of holding you again

Be prepared. Next time I won't let go, my Angel Prince and best friend.

L: for the love you brought into this world

One look at you and lost faith in humanity was instantly restored.

L: for Grandma Linda, oh, she misses you so.

Keep sending her love through lion sightings so forgiveness she'll know.

E: for eternity, that's how long our bond will last.

And thank God for that gift, 'cause Lord knows our time here ended too fast.

E: for every day I live to honor you

I promise I will make you proud if it's the only thing I do.

CHAPTER SEVEN

Reinvesting in Life

Reinvesting in Life

The thought of reinvesting in life can seem like we must leave our loved ones behind. That can be frightening and cause resistance. The purpose here is to inspire hope for healing and to provide guidance for adjusting to life without the physical presence of our loved ones. When speaking about readjusting, instead of "moving on" try the phrase "moving through" as it is more digestible. The word "on" seems final while "through" resonates as continuous. Facilitate an open discussion of their progress and challenges adapting to their new lives.

Activism can help us feel a new sense of purpose. My therapist suggested that I facilitate a support group for mothers whose babies are in the NICU. It did not sound appealing. The thought of it turned my stomach. At first, I felt guilty for not being eager to support them. Now, I feel settled about that not being a step on my path. Facilitating my "Good Grief" group, "spittin' poetry", and writing this guide are the options that fit my journey and soul. We do not have to feel guilty about honoring what is safe for us. Encourage members to identify ways they can turn their pain into passion. Have participants write at least one idea of how they can invest some of the love they have for their deceased loved one(s) into themselves, others, or the world.

Many of us wish we had a time machine that would take us back to before the death. Although I caution against ruminating on the past, reflecting with a new perspective can promote growth. Have clients consider what they would do or say if they could go back to the beginning of their grief journey and help themselves or loved ones. This can be written or openly talked about.

Underbelly

"If I Should Go Before You"

If I should go before you,

I've written a guide to help you through.

So, promise me my lady, this is what you'll do.

Morn if you must and cry.

But please don't die.

When you reach the bottom of the ocean remember the only place to go is up.

So, bend you knees and puuush with all your might and all your must.

I know how big a feat that would be, I was there once before myself.

So, promise me, before you stop on the tracks like me, you'll get some help.

Remember me, but don't focus on my death.

And loooove when you feel you have nothing left.

As time goes on, please allow yourself to smile

Even if it's only every once in a while.

When you start to doubt God, as it's likely you might

Remember he of all people understands as he too watched his child die.

Pick up the pieces and be alive each day.

Hope, believe, and continue to pray.

I'll talk to you often. When you can talk back.

That's how I'll know our love bond is still intact.

Yes, I'll be anxiously awaiting the next time we meet.

But please don't rush, I'll save you a seat.

As we neared the end of our group, I shared the ideas that grief is the physical expression of love that cannot be physically delivered, and tears are physical proof of love. These descriptions reminded members that grief is normal and expected when there is love. I referenced the T.E.A.R Model by J.W. Worden to sum up the process of death loss. These concepts soothed my members and may help bring solace to your group.

CHAPTER EIGHT

Release

Release

To live healthy lives through our grief journeys, we will have to release the parts of our bereavement that prevent us from healing. Be especially careful here. It is my personal and professional experience that people are likely to get offended when others suggest they let go of their deceased loved ones. Refrain from go to catchphrases like "forget the past" or "get over the past." The goal is to provide a framework of how members can continue to journey through life with exactly what they have: a nonphysical love relationship with the deceased.

To start the process, ask volunteers to share their "Love Creations" that were assigned as homework in the Commemorating session. Releasing this love may sufficiently inspire them to believe they can continue to heal. If the group desires to go further, balloon activities can be very symbolic and powerful. Your group may choose to design their own helium balloon release. "*Let It Out*" is a balloon release activity that I created. To facilitate this:

- pass out sharpies and balloons to each member

- have participants blow up a balloon and pinch the neck to keep the air in

- suggest they write their past and present grief feelings and thoughts on the balloon

- give the go ahead to release the air (if the balloons whiz off, have them retrieve theirs)

The words on the balloons will shrink. This signifies the power they possess. The emotions that fill them can be minimized if they choose to let them out. Even if air fills the balloons again, they always have the power to release. This activity can be modified to not require balloons. Simply have participants inhale their grief thoughts and feelings until their stomachs and chests fill, then exhale them all the way out by deflating their bodies. Repeat this cycle multiple times.

Underbelly

"Dandelions for my Dandy Lion"

I had a lion once upon a time.

He was surely dandy. I mean truly sublime.

Excellent, beautiful, and full of love,

but he was called to live with God above.

He left my care 4 years ago.

He didn't say goodbye, so I've had a hard time letting go.

Sometimes he speaks to me now, but I don't respond.

I've been punishing myself all along.

I want to talk back.

But "how to without breaking my own heart," my brain I rack.

The other day this thought came to my mind:

"I don't know if I can, but I'm ready to try.

I can't speak, so I'm going to blow dandelions to my guy.

And maybe, just maybe one will reach the sky."

I called my mom and shared the idea.

"I didn't realize the yellow flowers and the fuzzy ones were the same" she said.

I replied "yeah, you can only blow dandelions when they're dead."

As I approach the day I most dread,

I could spend this time crying and paining, but I'm going to play with my lion instead.

If you've lost a dandy lion of your own, please know that you are not alone.

I see you and I feel your pain. And I grieve with you always and especially on this day.

Join me if it's not too much.

Let's blow dandelions to our dandy lion cubs.

The grief process may not be linear. Different transitions and occurrences in life may require revisiting some of the topics explained in this guide. Taking steps backwards does not mean we are not "doing so good," which is a sentiment common to *grievers*. Seasonal depression and other recurring struggles are to be expected.

Request feedback and encouragers from members and facilitator(s). Allow members to exchange contact information if desired. Consider group input and, decide whether to reconvene. Remind members to reach out to family, friends and helpful resources when needed. Professional support information is listed in the resource section of this book. Mention them and provide members with a copy. Here's to healing and helping!

OTHERS

LIFE SAVERS

RECIPE FOR RELIEF

Measurement examples: cups, spoonful, pinch, dash, some, a little bit of, a lotta bit of

∧   _____

∧   _____

∧   _____

∧   _____

∧   _____

∧   _____

∧   _____

∧   _____

∧   _____

∧   _____

∧   _____

Suggested Readings

Tiny Beautiful Things: Advice of Love and Life from Dear Sugar by Cheryl Strayed

The Shack by William P. Young

References

Seven Stages of Grief Model by Elizabeth Kubler-Ross

Grief Share www.griefshare.org

T.E.A.R. Model of Grief by J.W. Worden

Tiny Beautiful Things: Advice of Love and Life from Dear Sugar by Cheryl Strayed

Ariel Perez Benino, illustrator of cover art

Resources

National Emergency Support Number: 911

National Suicide Prevention Hotline 1-800-273-8255

United Way (national grief and therapy resources): 211

Psychology Today (national grief and therapy resources): www.psychologytoday.com

Natalie Ross, LPC-S www.leenaenterprisesllc.com leenaenterprisesllc@gmail.com